D1523277

I See Squares

D.H. Dilkes

Bailey Books
an imprint of
Enslow Publishers, Inc.

New Hanover County Public Library
201 Chestnut Street
Wilmington, North Carolina 28401

Bailey Books, an imprint of Enslow Publishers, Inc.

Library of Congress Cataloging-in-Publication Data

Dilkes, D. H.

  I see squares / by D.H. Dilkes.

    p. cm. — (All about shapes)

  Includes index.

  Summary: "Simple text and photographs present a story with a theme about squares"—Provided by publisher.

  ISBN 978-0-7660-3802-8

  1. Square—Juvenile literature. 2. Shapes—Juvenile literature. I. Title.

  QA482.D537 2011

  516'.154—dc22

                        2010018403

Paperback ISBN: 978-1-59845-153-5

Printed in the United States of America

052010 Lake Book Manufacturing, Inc., Melrose Park, IL

10 9 8 7 6 5 4 3 2 1

To Our Readers: We have done our best to make sure all Internet Addresses in this book were active and appropriate when we went to press. However, the author and the publisher have no control over and assume no liability for the material available on those Internet sites or on other Web sites they may link to. Any comments or suggestions can be sent by e-mail to comments@enslow.com or to the address on the back cover.

Photo Credits: Shutterstock.com

Cover Photo: Shutterstock.com

Note to Parents and Teachers

Help pre-readers get a jumpstart on reading. These lively stories introduce simple concepts with repetition of words and short simple sentences. Photos and illustrations fill the pages with color and effectively enhance the text. Free Educator Guides are available for this series at www.enslow.com. Search for the *All About Shapes* series name.

Contents

Words to Know

cold   square

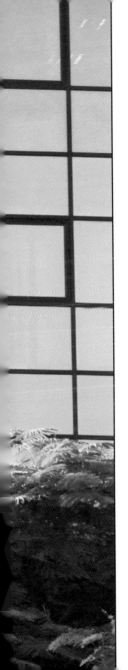

I see squares.

Some are cold.

Some are hot.

Some are old.

Some are not.

Where I wash.

Where I run.

Play in my home

or in the sun.

With you they
are fun.

Read More

Jones, Christianne C. *Four Sides the Same: A Book About Squares.* Minneapolis, Minn.: Picture Window Books, 2006.

Rau, Dana Meachen. *Squares.* New York: Marshall Cavendish Benchmark, 2007.

Web Sites

Fisher-Price. *Learn Your Colors and Shapes.*
<http://www.fisher-price.com/us/fun/games/colorshapes/>
Press any key to start!

Kids Learning Station. Preschool Shapes Worksheets.
<http://www.kidslearningstation.com/preschool/shapes -worksheets.asp>
Click on "Squares Worksheet."

Index

Guided Reading Level: B
Guided Reading Leveling System is based on the guidelines recommended by Fountas and Pinnell.

Word Count: 34

mL

S